AF316807

Girls Can SOAR!

Girls Can SOAR!

12 Life Habits

Andrea C. McLean

Girls Can SOAR!

Published in the United States of America

ISBN   Paperback: 979-8-9884568-0-3

ISBN   Hardback: 979-8-9884568-1-0

ISBN   eBook   979-8-9884568-2-7

DEDICATION

This book is dedicated to my daughter, daughter-in-law, and nieces. May you all continue to SOAR and achieve your dreams!

TABLE OF CONTENTS

INTRODUCTION

In a world filled with endless possibilities, girls today possess the extraordinary potential to achieve greatness and impact the world around them. Their dreams, aspirations, and innate talents can shape many lives, including their own. However, these bright lights get dimmed by self-doubt, fear, and a lack of self-belief. But now is the time for change. It's time for girls to break free from doubt and insecurity, spread their wings, and soar to new heights. It's time for them to speak up, advocate for themselves, and forge their paths in life.

"Girls Can SOAR!" is a book designed to empower girls and provide them with the tools, guidance, and inspiration they need to overcome obstacles, unleash their potential, and seize every opportunity that comes their way. This book is a compass, guiding them towards a future filled with confidence, resilience, and a strong belief in themselves to achieve anything they set their minds to do.

We will embark on a transformative journey together within the "Girls Can SOAR!" pages. We will explore 12 life habits integral to a girl's growth and success. We will delve into the power of self-belief and the importance of surrounding oneself with the right friends who uplift and inspire. We will learn to be organized, responsible, and proactive in pursuing our dreams while embracing the thrill of trying new things, appreciating our unique talents, and advocating for ourselves in every aspect of our lives.

We will also tackle the ever-present struggle girls face with self-doubt head-on and discover the strength to refuse to dwell on our mistakes, learn from them instead, and strive for improvement constantly. We will explore the transformative impact of reframing our self-talk and replacing negative thoughts with empowering positive ones that build rather than tear down. And when the journey becomes challenging, we will learn the art of asking for help while recognizing that this is a testament to our strength and willingness to grow.

Through practical advice and coaching, "Girls Can SOAR!" will empower girls to step into their power, awaken their potential, and ignite the flame of belief within themselves. This book will serve as a guiding light, reminding girls that they are worthy, capable, and deserving of all life's beautiful things.

So, let us embark on this empowering journey together. Let us dare to dream, break free from the constraints that hold us back, and embrace the limitless possibilities that await us. Whether you are a girl just starting on her journey or a young woman ready to grow and take the next step, this book is for you. You have the power to soar in life, and "Girls Can SOAR!" is here to help you every step of the way. Let's get started!

"Choose to soar. Choose to fly your dreams."

Jonathan Lockwood Huie

SOAR
The "S"

Speak Up & Use Your Voice

Stop Self-Doubt & Self-Criticism

Seek Out the Right Friends

"If you have the feeling that something is wrong, don't be afraid to speak up."

Fred Korematsu

CHAPTER 1

Speak Up & Use Your Voice

Are there times when you think you should speak up but don't? Do you ask yourself why that is the case? Is it that you are afraid that you will be judged by other people, you need to think more quickly on the spot, or you need to have more confidence that what you have to say is worthwhile?

Childhood experiences can cause fear of speaking up; for example, when you were in class, you raised your hand and gave the wrong answer and were embarrassed when your classmates laughed at you. Or you were reprimanded for speaking up by an adult. However, your voice and opinions do matter! You certainly have ideas and opinions that you want to express.

Learning to speak up for yourself is essential, which lets others know your thoughts and feelings. Keeping quiet is never a good idea, as silence can signal compliance. Here are some tips to speak up and use your voice:

1. Develop self-confidence. Build self-confidence and self-esteem to find and use your voice by recognizing your strengths, setting and achieving goals, celebrating your successes, and practicing positive self-talk. Feeling more confident may make you more likely to speak up and assert yourself.

2. Practice assertiveness. Express your opinions and needs clearly and respectfully. Practice using "I" statements to communicate your thoughts and feelings, e.g., "I am not comfortable doing that."

3. Seek opportunities to speak up. Participate in school or community events, volunteer, or join a club or organization to develop your communication skills and build confidence in your speaking ability.

4. Surround yourself with support. Finding supportive friends, family, and mentors who encourage you to express yourself can give you the encouragement and validation to speak up and assert yourself.

You can start to build the skill of speaking up by setting a goal to say something at least once daily in discussions with your friends and family. Every time you speak up, you should feel proud of yourself for being courageous. And as time passes, it will become much easier for you to do this. When girls speak up, they empower themselves and inspire others around them. By sharing their thoughts, ideas, and concerns, girls contribute to a diverse range of perspectives.

Moreover, as girls gain confidence in expressing their opinions, they develop essential leadership skills that can positively impact their personal and professional lives. Remember, your voice matters; using it can create a brighter future for yourself and others. Speak up, be heard, and use your voice for everyone's benefit!

Coaching Reflection

What do you think stops you from speaking up?

"You've been criticizing yourself for years and it hasn't worked. Try approving of yourself and see what happens."

Louise Hay

CHAPTER 2

Stop Self-Doubt & Self-Criticism

Self-doubt and self-criticism happen to all of us and typically begin in childhood. Sometimes it is from peer pressure, competitive sports, trying to excel in school, or even critical loved ones closest to us. There are times when self-doubt can be helpful by preventing you from making a wrong or bad decision. However, if you constantly doubt yourself, that can be a problem. Do you give yourself credit for doing things, or do you usually feel the need to improve? Self-doubt could likely be impacting your life in a negative and unhealthy manner.

Self-doubt can create a cycle of self-criticism. Over time this can impact your future goals and plans. The consequences of self-criticism include constantly comparing yourself to others and blaming yourself for negative situations that might be out of your control, which can impact your mental well-being. Many times, the thoughts and messages girls send to themselves are not true, harmful, or exaggerated. Here are six ways to combat self-doubt and self-criticism:

1. Recognize your best qualities. Remember what you do well, such as "I am a good listener," "I am responsible," "I am good at math," or "I am a good artist."

2. Search for proof. You got a B+ on an exam rather than an A. That doesn't mean you will fail the class. Your mind tells you things that aren't true all the time.

3. Replace self-critical ideas. Getting a B+ is still a good grade, even though you didn't do as well as you wanted. You still have more chances to perform well in the class.

4. Resist negative beliefs. When negative thoughts such as "I am a horrible person," "I look ugly," or "I am a failure." enter your head, ask yourself whether the thought is helpful to you.

5. Be kind to yourself. How would you react if a friend confided in you that they were having this unpleasant thought? Would you use such negative language with your friend?

Having and maintaining a good self-image and avoiding perfectionism empowers girls to embrace their unique selves, prioritize their well-being, pursue their goals, and lead fulfilling lives. By letting go of perfectionism, girls can liberate themselves from the pressure to meet impossible standards and instead focus on personal growth, resilience, and happiness. Accept yourself for who you are and readjust your thinking when needed. It's time to start believing in yourself.

Coaching Reflection

What are those situations where you are most critical of yourself?

"There's nothing like a really loyal, dependable, good friend. Nothing."
Jennifer Aniston

CHAPTER 3

Seek Out the Right Friends

Friendship is important in life. However, choosing the right friends is key to your well-being. You've probably heard your parents saying to be careful about whom you choose as friends because this can positively or negatively affect your life. Some friends are just not good influences, and they could do or say things that make you uncomfortable. For example, being mean to others or doing stuff you were taught is wrong to do.

The right friends should bring out the best in you. Here are six essential things you should look for when choosing friends:

1. Honesty. Do they tell you the truth or cover things up?

2. Values. Do they have similar values and standards?

3. Goals. Do their goals align with yours, e.g., graduating from high school or pursuing their dreams?

4. Strengths. Can they do some things better than you to help make up for what you're not good at?

5. Support. Do they motivate, encourage, and stand by you when needed?

6. Recognition. Do they applaud your success, or are they jealous when you do well?

If you notice any of the characteristics below, you are likely not surrounding yourself with the right friends:

1. Needy. Are they always looking to get something from you, but they never give in return?

2. Conditional. Do you have to do things for them to remain their friend?

3. Disrespectful. Are they disrespectful to you in person, or do they speak badly about you behind your back or on social media?

4. Untrustworthy. Do they break their promises to you?

5. Draining. Does being around them require lots of energy to deal with their drama?

It's time to reevaluate your friendships, even those you have had for a long time. Are these friends building you up or breaking you down? You must decide whether to keep these friends, as having the wrong friendships can be detrimental to your future.

Coaching Reflection

What are some friendships that you know aren't right for you?

SOAR
The "O"

Organize Your Tasks

Own Your Responsibilities

Open Yourself Up to Trying New Things

"Getting organized is a sign of self-respect."

Gabrielle Bernstein

CHAPTER 4

Organize Your Tasks

Being organized is a habit that we all should cultivate. If you have missed assignment deadlines, can't find important documents, or never seem to be able to get to places on time, getting organized should be a priority. There are great benefits to being organized, like increasing your productivity, reducing the stress you might feel if you're late with an assignment, and arriving on time at places you need to be. Here are some ways you can organize your tasks:

1. Create a to-do list. This will help you remember the important tasks and when to complete them.

2. Calendar the tasks. Put manageable tasks on your calendar to help you to stay on track.

3. Cross off tasks. You will have a feeling of accomplishment by crossing tasks off your to-do list as you complete them.

Here are seven practical ways to improve your organizational skills:

1. Clearly label your files and folders. You will find information more quickly whether the files are on your computer or in hard copy.

2. Try to keep things you use regularly in the same place. If, for example, you put your keys, backpack, cell phone, shoes, etc., in the same place, you will find it much faster to locate these items when needed.

3. Create a routine for yourself. Identify the tasks you can do at the same time every day to ensure they get completed.

4. Set your alarm clock for 10-15 minutes earlier. Giving yourself some extra time as a cushion will be helpful if you need it.

5. Lay out your clothes the night before. You won't have to spend time deciding what to wear in the morning.

6. Clear out your backpack at least every weekend. You won't keep unnecessary clutter, and you'll be able to find what you need quickly.

7. Make your bed. I know this isn't a popular thing these days, but you'd be amazed how much a made bed can create a sense of calm, plus you won't have items lost between the covers.

While organization may not come naturally to you, that doesn't mean you can't become more organized with practice. If you form good habits and establish a routine that you follow every day, you will be able to get your life and tasks in order, and as you continue to follow your routine, you will feel more organized.

Coaching Reflection

What are some areas where you know you need to be more organized?

____

____

____

____

____

____

____

____

"You must take personal responsibility. You cannot change the circumstances, the seasons, or the wind, but you can change yourself. That is something you have charge of."

Jim Rohn

CHAPTER 5

Own Your Responsibilities

Responsibility is one of the most essential traits we can have in our lives. It helps us to gain the skills we need to succeed and gives us the drive and determination always to do what is best. You can be responsible for yourself, others in your family, your friends, or anyone depending on you. Being responsible brings many benefits and can help you achieve your goals and become trustworthy while allowing you to have principles and beliefs by which you live your life. Here are some reasons why being responsible is essential:

1. **It helps you to get things done and meet your deadlines.**
2. **You become more confident in your abilities.**
3. **It helps to build your self-esteem.**
4. **It teaches you how to be accountable for your actions.**
5. **You are better at solving problems.**
6. **You improve your decision-making skills.**
7. **It teaches you about life and relationships.**
8. **It improves your reputation as a reliable person.**

When girls are responsible, they take ownership of their ideas, beliefs, goals, mistakes, and successes. Responsibility allows them to control their future by helping them grow and develop the skills and tenacity to succeed. You are accountable for your actions, dependable, and care for others. Of course, on the other hand, you also want to be careful not to be overly responsible for things that others should be doing or that are beyond your control. For example, are you always helping others to complete their assignments or feeling like you need to cover up someone else's mistake? Being responsible doesn't mean taking on everyone else's burdens. That, instead, is being over-responsible, so be careful to figure out the difference.

Making a choice is an essential component of individual responsibility. Every day you make conscious or unconscious decisions that affect how your life turns out. Some decisions are less significant than others, like what to eat for lunch versus whether to graduate high school or college. Your life will ultimately become a result of all your decisions, so accept your responsibility when making decisions.

Coaching Reflection

Where do you think you could be more responsible?

"Often you will end up loving the new things you try and even if you don't love it, you've given yourself a new experience."

Alli Simpson

CHAPTER 6

Open Yourself Up to Trying New Things

Trying something new is usually a good idea. You never know how you might open yourself up to new experiences, learn new things, and add some fun to your life. Of course, trying something new can also be difficult because you will be doing something that is unfamiliar. There are several important reasons why girls should try new things:

1. Personal growth and self-discovery. When girls try new things, they can find out that they like to do certain things or have a newfound passion. You learn more about yourself. Through new situations, you can find hidden talents and learn new skills, which helps you grow as a person.

2. Expanding horizons. When you try new things, you learn about other places, ways of thought, and points of view. Girls can get a fuller picture of the world and learn to be more understanding.

3. Building resilience and adaptability. Trying new things involves meeting challenges and getting out of your comfort zone. This makes girls more resilient because they learn to deal with problems, adjust to new settings, and solve problems. These traits are important for being successful in many areas of life. You might meet new people and create new friendships.

4. Getting over fears and building confidence. Trying new things can help girls overcome their fears, build confidence, and develop a "can-do" attitude. Every new thing you do gives you a chance to see that you can do well in situations that are new to you.

5. Finding new passions and interests. When girls try new things, they may find new passions and interests they didn't know about before. By trying out different things, hobbies, and experiences, you may find something that really excites you and makes you happy.

Exploring uncharted territories can awaken your senses, ignite your creativity, and unveil hidden talents you never knew you possessed. This can lead to personal growth, expand your perspective, and introduce you to diverse experiences that enrich your life. By stepping outside familiar routines, you open yourself up to the possibility of discovering untapped passions, forging new connections, and achieving extraordinary accomplishments. So, why not try something new, from a simple task to a more challenging one? You will reap the benefits and have much richer experiences in life.

Coaching Reflection

What are some new things you would like to try?

SOAR
The "A"

Appreciate Your Unique Gifts & Talents

Ask for Help When Needed

Advocate for Yourself

"It is time to recognize your gifts and talents, to appreciate and honor all that you do well."

Debbie Ford

CHAPTER 7

Appreciate Your Unique Gifts & Talents

We all have natural gifts and talents and there is no right or wrong gift or talent – you need to accept your unique skills and talents. You are born with them and naturally good at doing them. It is best not to compare your talents with someone else's talents, as you will lose self-confidence in your worth. What are those things that you like doing or that make you happy? Here are five important reasons to accept your unique skills and gifts:

1. Self-esteem and self-acceptance. Recognizing and appreciating your gifts and talents can improve self-esteem and help with self-acceptance. When girls know and accept their strengths, they feel good about themselves.

2. Personal fulfillment. Everyone has particular traits and skills that make them unique. Girls can do things and pursue goals that match their interests and abilities if they accept and develop their unique gifts. This can make you feel fulfilled, happy, and satisfied in your daily life.

3. Contribution to society. When girls accept and use their unique gifts and talents, they can make a positive difference in society. By showing off your skills and talents, you can motivate others and your communities and make a difference in the world.

4. Empowerment and resilience. Recognizing and using your unique gifts and talents can give you courage and the strength to face any challenges. You can use your strengths to get around problems and come up with creative answers.

5. Embracing variety. The unique skills and gifts of each person add to the rich tapestry of human diversity. By appreciating and celebrating your own differences, you can also do the same for the differences of others, which helps create a society of acceptance and respect.

Girls can reach their full potential, grow their interests, and live fulfilling lives that are true to who they are when they accept their unique gifts and skills. Begin by listing the things you like to do and ask supportive people as well for input. They might tell you something surprising that you didn't realize about yourself. Appreciate the unique gifts or abilities you have been given.

Coaching Reflection

What are some things that you are great at doing?

"There is no shame in asking for help; it is one of the most courageous things you'll ever do and will lead to greater connection with those around you."

Laura Lane

CHAPTER 8

Ask for Help When Needed

Have you ever felt embarrassed or afraid to ask for help? While you might view asking for help as being weak, it is a strength to realize where you might need support. This doesn't mean you aren't smart, a failure, or less competent than your friends. Even if you feel scared or demotivated, remember that other people need help, too, even if it's in a different way. Here are some reasons why asking for help is important:

1. Overcoming obstacles. Girls may face various challenges in life, such as academic difficulties, mental health issues, or personal problems. Asking for help from your teachers, parents, or professionals can help you overcome these obstacles and find solutions.

2. Building resilience. When girls ask for help, they learn to cope with adversity and develop resilience to bounce back from setbacks and challenges.

3. Learning new skills. Asking for help can allow girls to learn new skills and knowledge from mentors, coaches, or peers.

4. Fostering relationships. When girls ask for help, they build trust and strengthen relationships with others who can provide support and guidance.

5. Promoting mental health. Girls who seek help from trained professionals when struggling with mental health issues can receive the necessary care and treatment to improve their well-being and prevent further problems.

Accepting that you need help requires you to be courageous and vulnerable to admit you don't know everything or can't do it yourself. Here are ways to ask for help:

1. Evaluate what you need. It is essential to be clear when asking the other person to help you. For example, is it a skill-based need or an emotional need, etc.?

2. Find people who can help. Don't get discouraged if someone says no. Seek support from others.

3. Be respectful. It is a good idea to say please and thank you.

Asking for help is a great skill to cultivate, saving you time and unnecessary headaches in the long run. So, go ahead and get the help that you need.

Coaching Reflection

Whom could you ask for some help that you might need?

"Advocating for what you believe in is crucial - if you don't ask for it, people assume you don't need it!"

Karen Deitemeyer

CHAPTER 9

Advocate for Yourself

Girls can become self-advocates if they speak up about their wants and needs. Self-advocacy is important because it helps you get what you need, make your own decisions, learn to say "no" without feeling bad, set limits, and disagree respectfully. When advocating for yourself, it's important to be polite and show respect for others while expressing yourself with confidence. Girls can improve their ability to stand up for themselves and handle situations with clarity and grace if they learn to communicate well. Here are some things you can do:

1. Take a deep breath. When you need to advocate for yourself, the simple act of taking a deep breath to center your thoughts and emotions can help you regain composure, clarity, and confidence, enabling you to approach the situation more effectively.

2. Reflect on what just occurred. After an interaction or experience where you felt uncomfortable, take the time to reflect on the situation. Consider what happened, how you felt, and why you must address it.

3. Consider the things you want to change. Identify the areas or aspects you wish to see changed or improved. Communicate your needs to others by clearly defining what you want.

4. Speak slowly and clearly. When advocating for yourself, expressing your thoughts and needs is crucial. Speak slowly, enunciate your words, and use a confident tone.

5. Give the other person an opportunity to share their views. Advocating for yourself involves engaging in respectful dialogue. When expressing your needs, allow the other person to share their perspective.

6. Request assistance if everything stays the same. Sometimes, despite your best efforts, change may take time to occur. If you feel that your advocacy is not producing the desired outcomes, it is perfectly acceptable to ask for help from a trusted individual.

Recognize that no one is born knowing how to be their own self-advocate. It is a learned skill. When you learn to advocate for yourself, you will be better prepared to resolve problems, and you will also understand when help is needed to resolve an issue. By learning to advocate for yourself, you can feel empowered to change your world.

Coaching Reflection

What are some situations where you need to advocate for yourself?

SOAR
The "R"

Refuse to Dwell on Your Mistakes

Reframe Your Self-Talk

Realize Your Dreams by Setting Goals

"When you make a mistake, there are only three things you should ever do about it: admit it, learn from it, and don't repeat it."

Paul Bear Bryant

CHAPTER 10

Refuse to Dwell on Your Mistakes

We all make mistakes in life. While you might feel humiliated or regret the error, dwelling on past mistakes can be unproductive and detrimental to your well-being. The critical thing is to forgive yourself, learn from your mistakes, and move forward. Here are some practical ways to refuse to dwell on your mistakes:

1. Acceptance. Acknowledge that mistakes are a part of life and that everyone makes them.

2. Practice self-compassion. Be kind to yourself. Recognize that making mistakes is a human experience and doesn't define your worth or abilities.

3. Learn from the mistake. Instead of dwelling on the error, you can focus on the lessons you can glean from it.

4. Shift your perspective. Reframe your mindset by looking at mistakes as opportunities for growth and improvement.

5. Be realistic with yourself. Understand that achieving perfection is unattainable, and everyone is bound to make mistakes. Strive for progress rather than perfection.

6. Surround yourself with support. Seek the help of trusted friends, family, or a mentor who can provide encouragement and perspective.

7. Take positive action. Instead of ruminating on the mistake, channel your energy into positive action. Identify steps you can take to rectify the situation or prevent similar errors in the future.

8. Seek professional help when needed. If letting go of past mistakes significantly impacts your daily life, you might need guidance and strategies tailored to your situation.

You are not your mistake. While it is human nature to spend time and energy replaying your mistakes, dwelling on the mistake will only make things worse, and you can't change what happened in the past. So, it's time to stop beating yourself up, forgive yourself, reflect on the progress you've made, and move forward from the mistake.

Coaching Reflection

What are some mistakes you've made where you need to forgive yourself?

"Be very careful what you say to yourself because someone very important is listening . . . YOU!"

John Assaraf

CHAPTER 11

Reframe Your Self-Talk

When was the last time you listened to how you speak to yourself? Do you tear yourself down or build yourself up? It may be time to reframe your negative self-talk into positive self-talk and tell yourself supportive, kind, and encouraging words, even in a difficult situation.

Reframing negative self-talk is essential to help girls develop a more positive and compassionate mindset. Here are some strategies girls can use to reframe negative self-talk:

1. Identify negative self-talk patterns. Become aware of your negative self-talk patterns. This involves recognizing the negative thoughts and beliefs that arise in your mind. Awareness of these patterns allows you to begin to challenge and reframe them.

2. Question the evidence. Ask yourself if there is any proof that the negative views are true. Often, you will find that your negative self-talk is based on opinions or skewed thinking. Examine your bad thoughts with an open mind. You can ask yourself if there is another, more reasonable way to look at the situation or a better way to explain it.

3. Replace negative thoughts with positive ones. Once you have challenged any negative thoughts, you can replace them with positive and affirming thoughts. You can consciously focus on your strengths, achievements, and positive qualities. Affirmations and positive self-talk can help reinforce these new thoughts.

4. Practice self-compassion. You can practice self-compassion by treating yourself with kindness, understanding, and acceptance. Remember that everyone makes mistakes and that being imperfect is okay. Offering self-compassion can counteract negative self-talk with a more forgiving and supportive mindset.

5. Seek support. You can seek support from trusted friends, family members, or professionals if you find it challenging to reframe your negative self-talk on your own. Sometimes, talking to someone can provide a fresh perspective and offer helpful insights.

It's important to note that reframing negative self-talk takes practice and patience. With consistent effort and self-compassion, girls can gradually shift their mindset toward a more positive and empowering one. There are enough people in life who will say negative things about you, so don't join in with them. Be your best cheerleader.

Coaching Reflection

What are some negative things you tell yourself that are not true?

"Stay focused, go after your dreams, and keep moving toward your goals."

LL Cool J

CHAPTER 12

Realize Your Dreams by Setting Goals

What do you imagine or dream about doing or becoming in the future? To see those dreams come to pass, you'll need to set some goals to get you on the right path. Goals can be short-term, to be achieved in the next 3-6 months, and others can be longer-term, within the next 1-3 years. Here are some ways that making goals can help you reach your dreams:

1. Write down your dreams. Get precise about what you want to accomplish. Take time to reflect on your passions, interests, and aspirations. By identifying your dreams and what you truly want to achieve, you can clearly envision what you are working towards.

2. Break the dreams down into S.M.A.R.T. goals. Setting goals that align with your dreams will help you to achieve your objectives. You'll need to ensure that the goals are **S**pecific, **M**easurable, **A**ttainable, **R**ealistic, and **T**ime-bound. Setting unrealistic goals can often lead to disappointment and frustration.

3. Make a plan of action. Goals are where you want to end up, and tasks are how you get there. Listing the different tasks to meet your goals and setting deadlines for each step can serve as a roadmap.

4. Learn from your mistakes. Use setbacks or failures as a setup for future success by considering what you can do differently next time. Flexibility and adaptability are key to achieving dreams.

5. Stay motivated. Pursuing dreams can be challenging, and there may be obstacles along the way. You can stay motivated by reminding yourself of your aspirations and celebrating small achievements and progress. Also, ask friends, family, or a mentor for help to encourage and push you to keep going.

Setting goals and taking consistent action toward them can turn your dreams into reality. And it is helpful if you believe in yourself, stay committed, and stay resilient even when faced with challenges. You can make significant strides toward achieving your dreams with determination and perseverance. Setting goals can keep you focused, inspired, and on track. I am excited about what you can achieve and will be cheering behind the scenes for you!

Coaching Reflection

What are some dreams and goals you have for the future?

CONCLUSION

As we end this empowering journey, I hope you, the reader, have gained a newfound sense of confidence and determination. Throughout this book, we explored 12 life habits of personal growth and self-empowerment essential for girls to SOAR.

You have learned the importance of speaking up and advocating for yourself. Your voice matters, and your opinions count. Remember that you can make a difference in your life and your world.

We have also discussed the significance of surrounding yourself with the right friends. Choose those who uplift and inspire you, believe in your dreams, and encourage you to pursue them. The people you surround yourself with can profoundly impact your self-belief and success.

Being organized and responsible has been emphasized as vital skills for achieving your goals. By managing your time effectively and staying on top of your commitments, you can create a solid foundation for success. Remember, every step forward, no matter how small, brings you closer to realizing your dreams.

Furthermore, we explored the importance of embracing new experiences and appreciating your talents. Don't be afraid to step out of your comfort zone, try new things, and discover hidden talents within yourself.

Celebrate your uniqueness and nurture your strengths; they are the key to unlocking your full potential.

Throughout this journey, we have acknowledged the inevitable reality of making mistakes. However, rather than dwelling on them, we have focused on the power of resilience and self-reflection. By reframing your self-talk and learning from your missteps, you can transform setbacks into opportunities for growth.

Additionally, we emphasized seeking help and guidance when needed. Asking for support is not a sign of weakness but a display of strength and wisdom. Remember that there are people around you who care and are willing to lend a helping hand. You are never alone on this journey.

Now, armed with knowledge, strategies, and a renewed belief in yourself, it is time for you to take flight. Trust in your abilities, trust in your dreams, and trust in the remarkable potential within you. With determination, perseverance, and a resilient spirit, you have the power to shape your destiny.

May this book serve as a guiding light, reminding you that you can overcome any obstacle and achieve the extraordinary. So, embrace your unique journey, and let your dreams SOAR high. The world is waiting for the incredible woman you will become!

Coaching Reflection

What is your favorite letter in SOAR, and your biggest takeaway?

ADDITIONAL COACHING RESOURCE

Girls Can SOAR!

Hello Reader,

*If you found this book beneficial, sign up for the companion **Girls Can SOAR! Virtual Coaching Course** with additional coaching content to help you soar in life at:*

https://acmcoachinggroup.thinkific.com/courses/girls-can-soar

My best to you,

Andrea C. McLean

MA, BCC, CPEC

ABOUT THE AUTHOR

Andrea C. McLean is a highly accomplished, board-certified life, career, and executive coach. With a global focus on leadership development, Andrea specializes in mentoring diverse women leaders in corporate and university settings. Her mission is to empower individuals to embrace their authentic selves, leverage their strengths, and overcome life's challenges to create a transformative path toward personal success.

Andrea's coaching approach is encouraging and inspiring, driven by a deep passion for helping others achieve their full potential. From her own experiences of loss and personal hardships, Andrea embodies resilience, grit, and a growth mindset, which she applies to her coaching practice. These life lessons have also motivated her to share her wisdom and insights through her books.

As an extraordinary coach, Andrea possesses a unique global perspective. During her sessions, she creates a psychologically safe and thoughtful environment where clients can explore their desires and aspirations. Andrea's expertise and guidance will propel you toward the next steps on your personal transformation journey. To discover more about Andrea and her coaching, please visit www.acmcoachinggroup.com to embark on a transformative experience with Andrea as your coach and unlock your true potential for success.

MORE BOOKS BY ANDREA C. McLEAN

The acronym FLAP stands for Face Life's Adversities and Persevere. This book shares inspiring stories of people who have overcome challenges to find success and offers encouragement and coaching questions for the reader.

This book is an inspirational story about a little girl named Andy who is trying to figure out what she should be when she grows up. The book encourages us to remember to look for the clues in our gifts and talents to point us in a career direction.

www.ingramcontent.com/pod-product-compliance
Lightning Source LLC
Chambersburg PA
CBHW050741150726
48196CB00003B/298